# SCHOLASTIC
## ENGLISH SKILLS

D0527353

# Comprehension
# Workbook

Ages
10–11

# SCHOLASTIC
## ENGLISH SKILLS

# Comprehension

Scholastic Education, an imprint of Scholastic Ltd
Book End, Range Road, Witney, Oxfordshire, OX29 0YD
Registered office: Westfield Road, Southam,
Warwickshire CV47 0RA
www.scholastic.co.uk

© 2016, Scholastic Ltd

5 6 7 8 9   8 9 0 1 2 3 4 5

British Library Cataloguing-in-Publication Data
A catalogue record for this book is available from the British Library.

ISBN 978-1407-14182-4

Printed and bound in India by Replika Press Pvt. Ltd.

### Acknowledgements

The publishers gratefully acknowledge permission to reproduce the following copyright material: **Andersen Press** for the use of an extract from *Way Home* by Libby Hathorn. Text © 1994, Libby Hathorn. Illustration © 1994, Gregory Rogers. (1994, Mark Macleod, Random House Australia Pty); text and illustration from *The Steadfast Tin Soldier* by Naomi Lewis. Text © 1986, Naomi Lewis. Illustration © 1991, P.J. Lynch. (1991, Andersen Press Ltd). **Anness Publishing** for the use of two extracts from *A Child's Treasury of Classic Stories* retold by Nicola Baxter. Text © 2012, Nicola Baxter. Illustrations © 2012, Jenny Thorne. (2012, Anness Publishing Ltd). **Christian Aid** for the use of text and images from the Christian Aid Week Appeal 2015, *The Big Issue*. **Classical Comics Ltd** for the use of two extracts from *A Christmas Carol: The Graphic Novel* by Charles Dickens, adapted by Sean Michel Wilson. © 2008, Classical Comics Ltd. (2008, Classical Comics Ltd). **Dorling Kindersley Ltd** for the use of text and illustrations from *Evolution Revolution* by Robert Winston. © 2009, Dorling Kindersley Ltd. (2009, DK Publishing). **Faber and Faber Ltd** for the use of the cover illustration and text from *Rooftoppers* by Katherine Rundell. © Katherine Rundell, 2013. (2013, Faber and Faber Ltd). **John Foster** for the use of the poem 'Giant Winter' from the collection *Four O'Clock Friday* by John Foster. © 1991, John Foster. (1991, Oxford University Press). **Frances Lincoln Children's Books** for the use of text and illustrations from *Azzi In Between* by Sarah Garland. Text and illustrations © 2012, Sarah Garland. (2012, Frances Lincoln Children's Books); the poem 'Kite Flying' by Debjani Chatterjee and an illustration from the collection *Let's play*, edited by Debjani Chatterjee and Brian D'Arcy, illustrated by Shirin Adl. Poem © 2013, Debjani Chatterjee. Anthology © 2013, Frances Lincoln Ltd. (2013, Frances Lincoln Ltd). Scriptures taken from the Holy Bible, New International Version®, NIV®. © 1973, 1978, 1984, 2011, Biblica Inc.™ Used by permission of Zondervan. www.zondervan.com. **Nosy Crow Ltd** for the use of an extract from *The Secret Hen House Theatre* by Helen Peters. Text © 2012, Helen Peters. Cover photograph © 2012, Marsha Arnold. (2012, Nosy crow Ltd). **Orion Children's Books** for the use of text from *Dead Man's Cove* by Lauren St John. Text © 2010, Lauren St John. (2010, Orion Children's Books); text and an illustration from *Tinder* by Sally Gardner, illustrated by David Roberts. Text © 2013, Sally Gardner. Illustration © 2013, David Roberts. (2013, Orion Children's Books). **Oxford University Press** for the use of the cover illustration from *After Tomorrow* by Gillian Cross. Text © 2013, Gillian Cross. (2013, Oxford University Press); text and an illustration from *The River Singers* by Tom Moorhouse. Text © 2013, Tom Moorhouse. Illustrations © 2013, Simon Mendez. (2013, Oxford University Press). **Macmillan Children's Books** for the use of text and an illustration from *Alienography* by Chris Riddell. © 2010, Chris Riddell. (2010, Macmillan Children's Books). **Penguin Random House UK** for the use of text from *Mercedes Ice* by Philip Ridley, illustrated by Chris Riddell. Text © 1996, Philip Ridley. (1996, Puffin Books). **The Random House Group Ltd** for the use of the cover illustration and a text extract from *The Casebooks of Captain Holloway: The Disappearance of Tom Pile* by Ian Beck. Text © 2015, Ian Beck. (2015, Corgi Children's). **Scholastic Children's Books** for the use of text and illustrations from *Horrible Geography of the World* by Anita Ganeri. Text © 2007, Anita Ganeri. Illustrations © 2007 Mike Phillips. (2007, Scholastic Ltd). **Usborne Publishing** for the use of text and illustrations from *50 Science Things to Make and Do*. © 2008, 2005 Usborne Publishing Ltd. (2008, Usborne Publishing Ltd); text and illustrations from *Little Encyclopedia of Science*. © 2006, Usborne Publishing Ltd. (2006, Usborne Publishing Ltd). **Walker Books Ltd** for the use of text and illustration from *Tales from Shakespeare* by Marcia Williams. Text and illustrations © 2014, Marcia Williams. (2014, Walker Books Ltd); text and an illustration from *Great Explorers* by Stewart Ross, illustrated by Stephen Biesty. Text © 2011, Stewart Ross. Illustrations © 2011, Stephen Biesty. (2011, Walker Books Ltd); text and illustrations from *Mysterious Traveller* by Mal Peet and Elspeth Graham, illustrated by P.J. Lynch. Text © 2013, Mal Peet and Elspeth Graham. Illustrations © 2013, P.J. Lynch. (2013, Walker Books Ltd); text and illustration from *Bravo, Mr William Shakespeare!* by Marcia Williams. Text and illustrations © 2000, Marcia Williams. (2000, Walker Books Ltd). **Wildlife Watch**, The Wildlife Trusts for the use of an activity sheet from www.wildlifewatch.org.uk. © 2015, Royal Society of Wildlife Trusts. Illustrations © 2015, Corinne Welch.

Every effort has been made to trace copyright holders for the works reproduced in this book, and the publishers apologise for any inadvertent omissions.

### Images

Page 23, Bones and muscles. © Puwadol Jaturawutthichai/shutterstock.com. Page 28, There is a Time. © Digiselector/shutterstock.com. Page 35, What the Dickens. © Everett Historical. Page 47, Giant Winter. © Triff/shutterstock.com, © Rena Kuljovska/shutterstock.com. Page 67, Weather. © PhotographByMK/shutterstock.com, © Melanie Lynn Freelance/shutterstock.com, © Irina BG/shutterstock.com.

**Author** Donna Thomson
**Editorial** Rachel Morgan, Anna Hall, Kate Soar, Margaret Eaton
**Consultants** Hilarie Medler, Libby Allman

**Cover and Series Design** Neil Salt and Nicolle Thomas
**Layout** K & S Design
**Illustration** Gemma Hastilow-Smith
**Cover Illustration** Eddie Rego

# Contents

# How to use this book

- *Scholastic English Skills Workbooks* help your child to practise and improve their skills in English.

- The content is divided into chapters that relate to different skills. The final 'Review' chapter contains a mix of questions that bring together all of these skills. These questions increase in difficulty as the chapter progresses.

- Keep the working time short and come back to an activity if your child finds it too difficult. Ask your child to note any areas of difficulty. Don't worry if your child does not 'get' a concept first time, as children learn at different rates and content is likely to be covered at different times throughout the school year.

- Find out more information about comprehension skills and check your child's answers at www.scholastic.co.uk/ses/comprehension.

- Give lots of encouragement, complete the 'How did you do' for each activity and the progress chart as your child finishes each chapter.

**Topic**
The topic you are working on.

**Activity title**
The title of the activity.

**Instruction**
The instruction tells you what to do.

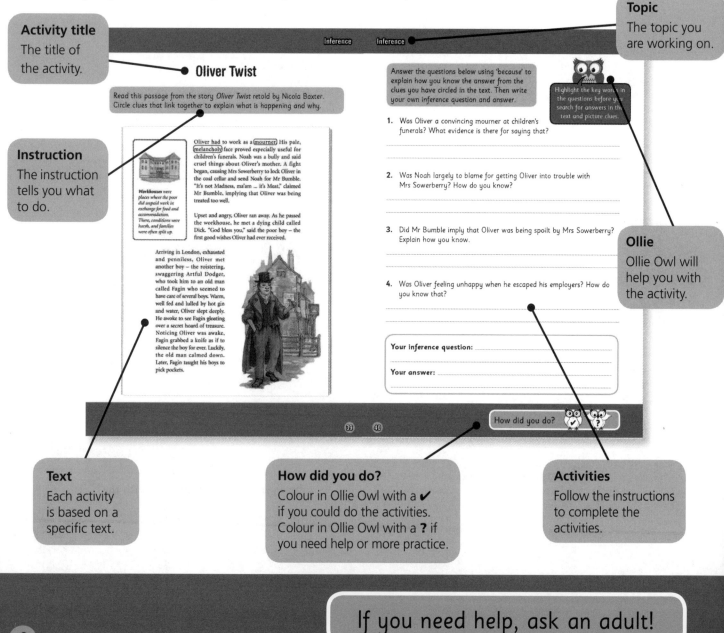

**Ollie**
Ollie Owl will help you with the activity.

**Text**
Each activity is based on a specific text.

**How did you do?**
Colour in Ollie Owl with a ✔ if you could do the activities. Colour in Ollie Owl with a **?** if you need help or more practice.

**Activities**
Follow the instructions to complete the activities.

If you need help, ask an adult!

# Antony and Cleopatra

Read the beginning of *Antony and Cleopatra* by Shakespeare, retold by Marcia Williams.

**Who** is in the story? **What** are they doing? **Where** are they?

Three men, Mark Antony, young Octavius Caesar and Aemilius Lepidus once ruled the Roman world. Caesar and Lepidus took care of the affairs of state in Italy, but Antony made merry in Egypt.

Antony was in love with Egypt's queen, Cleopatra, and could not bear to leave her.

But news came that his wife, Fulvia, had died and his power in Rome was weakening.

In spite of Cleopatra's pleas, Antony and his good friend, Enobarbus, left for Rome.

Caesar and Lepidus resented the time the once noble Antony spent in Egypt, and despised his neglect of duty.

In order to strengthen his alliance with the two leaders once more, Antony agreed to marry Caesar's sister, Octavia.

Use different coloured pens to highlight the 'who', 'what' and 'where' information in the text on page 5. Some examples have been done for you. Then use the information you've underlined to help you retell the beginning of the story in your own words.

The answers are right there in the pictures and text.

Once there were _____

_____

_____

_____

_____

_____

Read the text again and answer the questions below. Then ask and answer your own 'who', 'what' and 'where' questions about the text.

**1.** What is the theme of this story?

_____

**2.** Who left Egypt to go to Rome with his good friend?

_____

**3.** Where were Caesar and Lepidus while Antony was away?

_____

**4.** What were Caesar and Lepidus doing while Antony was away?

_____

_____

**5.** Where did Antony fall in love?

_____

**6.** Who did Antony agree to marry?

_____

**7.** What happened when Antony fell in love with Cleopatra?

_____

_____

_____

**Your 'who' question:** _____

_____

**Your answer:** _____

_____

**Your 'what' question:** _____

_____

**Your answer:** _____

_____

**Your 'where' question:** _____

_____

**Your answer:** _____

_____

How did you do?

# Working with Nature

Read this extract from *Working with Nature*.

**Who** and **what** is this information about? What's the problem? How is it solved?

## Protecting wildlife

Many crop farmers leave a wide band of natural vegetation round the edge of their fields. Along with hedges, trees and woods, these pesticide-free wildlife reserves are rich in the grasses and flowers that provide food sources and shelter for insects and animals.

**Frogs**
Populations of frogs help farmers to control slugs – a major crop pest.

**Hedgehogs**
In natural areas, hedgehogs flourish and prey on slugs and insects.

**Birds**
Thrushes and other birds thrive on wild areas of farmland, where they feed on snails and insects.

Many farmers in the developed world are turning away from using pesticides and fertilizers and are growing food more naturally. Organic farming produces smaller harvests than intensive farming and, as a result, produce can be more expensive. However, some consumers are happy to pay a bit extra in return for chemical-free foods. Farmers in developing countries with poor soils can also increase their food production by growing combinations of crops. This farming method protects the land by putting nutrients back into the soil, and also conserves the environment.

## Action!

Start a compost heap at home to save on plan fertilizer and improve the soil in your garden.

See what organic foods are available in your local supermarket. Meat and dairy products can be organic, too.

Animal manure can be sprayed from a tank mounted on a tractor.

Identify the problems mentioned in *Working with Nature*. Find and underline the solutions to complete the table below. An example has been done for you. Then use the clues you have underlined to help you answer the questions on page 10.

| Problem | Solution |
|---|---|
| Pesticides are a danger to wildlife. | Many crop farmers leave natural vegetation round the edge of their fields to provide pesticide-free food sources and shelter for wildlife. |
| | |
| | |
| | |
| | |
| | |

1. Explain the problem with pesticides in the developed world and what farmers are doing to find a solution.

   _____

   _____

   _____

2. What is the main problem with organic farming?

   _____

   _____

3. What are developing countries doing to solve the problem of poor soil and food production?

   _____

   _____

4. What do frogs and hedgehogs do to help farmers?

   _____

   _____

5. How can you cheaply and effectively improve the soil in your garden?

   _____

   _____

6. In your own words, retell who has problems with farming and how they solve them.

   _____

   _____

   _____

   _____

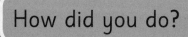 How did you do?

# How to be a snake charmer

Read the instructions below that tell you how to be a snake charmer.

## Be a snake charmer

Experiment with static electricity in this charming chapter.

1. Put a plate on a piece of tissue paper and draw around it. Cut out the circle. Draw a spiral snake inside it, like this.

2. To decorate your snake, draw a zigzag pattern and eyes with felt-tip pens. Then cut along the spiral.

3. Rub a plastic ruler fairly hard and fast for half a minute with a scarf or sweater made from wool.

4. Then touch the snake's head with your ruler. Slowly lift the ruler. The snake should uncoil and rise up.

### What's going on?

When the wool is rubbed against the plastic ruler, it causes particles too small to see to pass from the wool to the ruler. These extra particles on the ruler cause a build-up of static electricity, The static pulls on the tissue paper. The tissue paper is so light that the static on the ruler is strong enough to lift it.

As you rub the ruler, it gains extra particles.

The particles are transferred from the wool.

List the items you need to be a snake charmer.

1. _____
2. _____
3. _____
4. _____
5. _____
6. _____

Retell the instructions from page 11 in your own words and answer the questions below. Then ask and answer your own question about the text.

**First:** _____

_____

**Then:** _____

_____

**Next:** _____

_____

**Finally:** _____

_____

1.  What area of science is experimented with in this activity?

_____

2.  When do the instructions tell you to rub a plastic ruler with something woollen? Explain why you need to do this for this experiment to work.

_____

_____

_____

**Your question:** _____

_____

**Your answer:** _____

_____

_____

How did you do?

# Azzi In Between

Read this page from the story *Azzi In Between*.

Who is this story about? What is the **problem**? How is the problem **resolved**?

Grandma was very tired, but after supper she told them her story.

"Bad men came to the house with guns. I was very frightened.

I had to leave everything. Our beautiful home, the garden, the chickens.

I sold my golden bracelets to pay for my journey.

I travelled by night in a big lorry. It was hard and dangerous.

During the day, we had to stop and hide ourselves away.

When I arrived here I was afraid they would send me back.

I felt so happy when they told me I could stay.

We are safe for now and we are together, that's all that matters," said Grandma.

Look carefully at the pictures on page 13 and read the text again. Write the beginning, middle and end of Grandma's story in your own words and in the correct order.

**Beginning:** The story is about... (Who? What? Where?)

**Middle:** The problem is...

**End:** I think what happens in the end is...

How did you do?

# Hamlet, Prince of Denmark

Read this extract from *Hamlet, Prince of Denmark.*

Red pen for **who**.
Blue pen for **what**.
Green pen for **where**.

*Long ago in Denmark, the ghost of a man was seen to walk the high, bleak, windswept battlements of Elsinore Castle.* He uttered not a word and his footsteps made no sound against the crashing of the surf on the cliffs below. Twice now, the night guards had reported seeing the ghostly figure walk silently along the battlements. He was dressed in full armour and a long cloak whipped the wind behind him. The guards were certain he was not a figment of their imagination. Indeed, they believed he was the spirit of their late king.

The king had been dead for two months and good sense told the guards that his spirit would not return to haunt them, yet they could not shake the idea. Brave as they were, the night soldiers trembled with fear at the unnatural sight. The phantom looked so sad and troubled, but he would not speak, even when a watchman cried out, "What art thou? By heaven, I charge thee, speak!"

Hamlet, Prince of Denmark, son of the late king and heir to his crown, had idolized his father and was completely devastated by his sudden death. His father had been bitten by a serpent while sleeping in his orchard, so his death was unexpected and untimely. The old king had been a great monarch, loved and honoured by all the people of Denmark.

Highlight the 'who', 'what' and 'where' information in the text in different coloured pens. Then put the information in the table below. An example has been done for you.

The literal answers are right there in the text.

| Who | What (doing) | Where |
|---|---|---|
| The ghost of a man | was seen to walk | the high, bleak, windswept battlements of Elsinore Castle in Denmark. |
|  |  |  |
|  |  |  |
|  |  |  |

Read the text again and then answer the questions below.

**1.** What was the ghost of a man seen doing at Elsinore Castle, Denmark?

_____

**2.** Who had reported seeing the ghostly figure?

_____

**3.** Where was Hamlet's father when he was bitten by a serpent?

_____

Now ask and answer your own 'who', 'what' and 'where' questions, using the information in the table on page 16.

**Your 'who' question:** _____

**Your answer:** _____

_____

**Your 'what' question:** _____

**Your answer:** _____

_____

**Your 'where' question:** _____

**Your answer:** _____

_____

**Your question:** _____

**Your answer:** _____

_____

**Your question:** _____

**Your answer:** _____

_____

How did you do?

# The Secret Hen House Theatre

Read this extract from *The Secret Hen House Theatre*. Then re-read it and highlight the characters (nouns), actions (verbs) and places (nouns) in different coloured pens. An example has been done for you.

Use red pen for characters (**who/what** it is about). Use blue pen for action (**what** they are doing). Use green pen for places (**where** they are).

BANG, BANG, BANG!

Somebody was trying to smash the scullery door down.

Hannah sat cross-legged on her bedroom floor, hunched over a piece of paper, her pen racing across the page. Even inside the farmhouse her breath came out in white trails, and the cold sneaked its way right through her woolly hat and three jumpers.

BANG, BANG, BANG!

Her right hand didn't leave the page as she glanced at her watch. Five to two. But it couldn't be Lottie. She never knocked. She just walked right in and yelled up the stairs.

One of the others could get it for once. She had to finish this by two o'clock.

BANG, BANG, BANG!

"Will someone answer that blasted door!" shouted her dad from the farm office.

There! Finished at last. Hannah wrote "THE END" in large capital letters. This play would win the competition, she just knew it.

BANG, BANG, BANG!

Use the information you have highlighted on page 18 to answer these questions. Then ask and answer your own literal questions.

The literal answers are right there in the text.

**1.** Who was cold even inside the farmhouse?

_____

**2.** What was Hannah doing in her bedroom?

_____

**3.** Where was Hannah's dad while she was writing?

_____

**4.** What made her dad shout?

_____

**Your literal question:** _____

**Your answer:** _____

_____

**Your literal question:** _____

**Your answer:** _____

_____

**Your literal question:** _____

**Your answer:** _____

_____

How did you do?

# Mercedes Ice

Read the text from *Mercedes Ice* by Philip Ridley.

This is how it happened:

Doll, Rosie's mother, <u>was sitting in her hospital bed</u>. <u>In her arms was the newborn Rosie</u>.

Suddenly the air was full of noises: screeching and roaring like approaching monsters. Birds flew from trees and dogs started to bark.

Rosie cried.

'Hush now,' said Doll, rocking her daughter. 'It's nothing, sweetheart. Nothing.'

But the noises got louder and louder.

Rosie's cries turned to screams.

Doll was worried as well. She had never heard anything like it before. She turned to the woman in the next bed and asked, 'What is it, do you think?'

The woman, a tall, thin, stick of a thing, was holding a baby as well. His name was Timothy.

'Oh, they're digging foundations,' said Timothy's mother. 'Next to the school.'

Read these literal questions. Search the text for the underlined words in the questions. Use the information nearby to answer the questions.

**Example:**

**Question:** Who was <u>sitting in her hospital bed</u> with her <u>newborn in her arms</u>?

**Answer:** Doll, Rosie's mother was sitting in her hospital bed with her newborn in her arms.

1. What were the <u>noises</u> that made <u>Rosie's cries turn to screams</u>?

_____

2. Who <u>had never heard anything like it before</u>?

_____

Answers to **literal** questions are right there in the text and pictures.

Read the text and look at the picture from the next page in the story. Then answer the questions on page 22.

'Foundations for what?' asked Doll.

'A tower block,' replied Timothy's mother. 'It's going to be the tallest building in the whole area. When it's finished the top will touch the clouds.'

That night, Harold, Doll's husband, came to the hospital to look at Rosie. He gave Doll a bunch of grapes and a pretty card that had 'Well Done' written on it.

Then another man came into the ward. He was tall and muscular and had shining black hair. He walked over to the bed next to Doll and kissed Timothy's mother.

'Dearest!' he exclaimed.

Then he gave Timothy's mother, whose name was Sandra, a brown paper bag.

Inside were shrimps and shellfish and pickled herring.

Doll pinched her nose and said, 'Oh, what a stink!'

Search for key words that are the same in the question and in the text.

Underline the key words in these questions and find them in the text on page 21. The answers will be nearby. Then ask and answer your own literal question.

**Example:**

**Question:** Who said <u>the tower block top will touch the clouds</u>?

**Answer:** Timothy's mother said the tower block top will touch the clouds.

1. What did Harold do when he came to the hospital to look at Rosie?

_____

2. Who came into the ward and kissed Timothy's mother?

_____

3. What did the tall muscular man do after he exclaimed 'Dearest!'

_____

4. Who said 'Oh, what a stink!' after Sandra opened the bag?

_____

Your literal question: _____

_____

Your answer: _____

_____

How did you do?

# Bones and muscles

**Skim** and **scan** the text below to find these key words and phrases. Underline each one as you find it. The first one has been done for you.

Tibia    bones meet    cartilage    collar    shin    different positions
squashed    move    without    protect    support system    blade

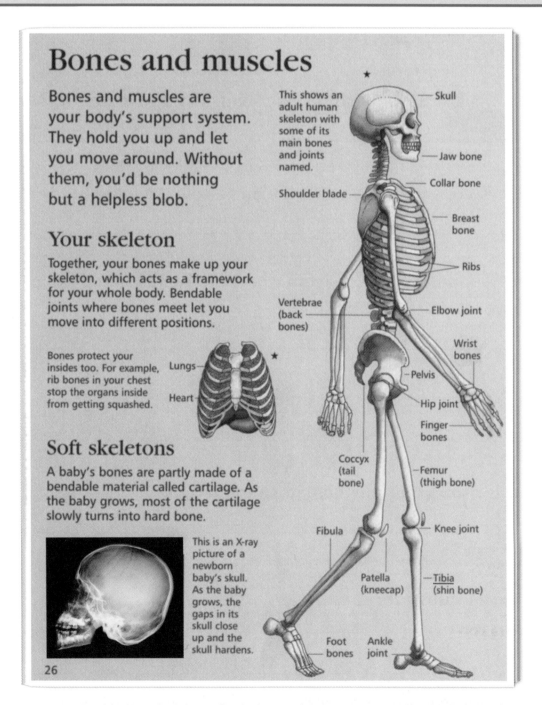

## Bones and muscles

Bones and muscles are your body's support system. They hold you up and let you move around. Without them, you'd be nothing but a helpless blob.

### Your skeleton

Together, your bones make up your skeleton, which acts as a framework for your whole body. Bendable joints where bones meet let you move into different positions.

Bones protect your insides too. For example, rib bones in your chest stop the organs inside from getting squashed.

Lungs

Heart

### Soft skeletons

A baby's bones are partly made of a bendable material called cartilage. As the baby grows, most of the cartilage slowly turns into hard bone.

This is an X-ray picture of a newborn baby's skull. As the baby grows, the gaps in its skull close up and the skull hardens.

This shows an adult human skeleton with some of its main bones and joints named.

Skull

Jaw bone

Collar bone

Shoulder blade

Breast bone

Ribs

Vertebrae (back bones)

Elbow joint

Wrist bones

Pelvis

Hip joint

Finger bones

Coccyx (tail bone)

Femur (thigh bone)

Fibula

Knee joint

Patella (kneecap)

Tibia (shin bone)

Foot bones

Ankle joint

26

Skim and scan the text for the words in bold in the following questions. Use these bold words and the words you have underlined to answer the questions about your body's support system. Then ask and answer your own literal question about the text.

Search for key words that are the same in the question and in the text.

1. What provides your body with **support** and enables you to **move** around?

   _____

2. What would happen **without** your body's **support system**?

   _____

3. Where is your **collar** bone in relation to your shoulder **blade**?

   _____

4. Name four parts of the skeleton where the **bones meet** and allow you to move into **different positions**.

   a. _____    b. _____    c. _____    d. _____

5. Give the other name for the **tibia**.

   _____

6. What is **protected** from getting **squashed**?

   _____

   **Your literal question:** _____

   **Your answer:** _____

   _____

How did you do?

# On the Roof of the World

Read this information about preparations for the British climbing expedition in Nepal that led to Tenzing Norgay and Edmund Hillary successfully scaling Mount Everest in 1953.

Think about the consequences of the planners' actions as you read.

Hunt was an experienced soldier who knew the vital importance of preparation and planning. To allow for sickness and injury, he chose a very large team of ten climbers, including two New Zealanders, George Lowe and Edmund Hillary. When they reached Nepal, the men would be joined by a group of experienced Sherpas, led by Tenzing Norgay.

The party chose and tested their equipment carefully. Modern materials helped them. Strong light nylon windproofed the climbers' padded clothing. Their boots were soled with flexible rubber rather than traditional leather, and lightweight aluminium was used for the frames of their backpacks and for the expedition's ladder.

Hunt understood the importance of diet, too. Griffith Pugh, one of the expedition doctors, calculated the number of calories each climber would need on the mountain, and made up army-style ration packs. At lower and middle altitudes, he knew, the men would have enormous appetites. At great heights, where their bodies needed food and liquid most, they would hardly want to eat or drink at all. In such circumstances, high-energy sugar, jam, biscuits and sweets were best, washed down with hot drinks of soup, cocoa and lemonade.

Hunt planned to pitch a series of camps up the mountain, perhaps as many as eight. Each would be well stocked with food, fuel, sleeping bags, oxygen and climbing gear. From the highest, he hoped to send out two or possibly three assault parties at the end of May. If the climbers were fit and the weather good, he hoped that one of these might reach the summit.

Underline clues in the text that suggest what might have happened to the mountaineers if health and safety precautions had not been so carefully considered by John Hunt, the leader of the expedition.

Using the information you have underlined, write one point that you consider vital when preparing a mountaineering expedition. Explain how it might affect the health or safety of the climbers. An example answer has been done for you.

This happened (effect) **because** of that (cause).

### Example:

Equipment: I think preparation of equipment by all the climbers is vital because it means everyone is familiar with the kit and confident that it is safe and easy to use before they set out.

_____

_____

_____

_____

_____

Using the information you have underlined, answer these questions about the causes and effects of planning for an expedition. Then ask and answer your own prediction question.

1.  What do you think might have happened if a less experienced person had led the Mount Everest expedition in 1953? Why do you think that?

_____

_____

_____

**2.** Do you think the mountaineers' plans changed at all as the expedition progressed? Why do you think that?

_____

_____

_____

**3.** Why do you think equipment made of modern materials might have been more helpful to the mountaineers than earlier climbing equipment?

_____

_____

_____

**4.** What do you think might have happened to other Everest mountaineers who did not have Griffith Pugh's 'ration packs'? Why do you say that?

_____

_____

**5.** Why do you think Norgay and Hillary found the last stage of the climb to the summit of Mount Everest more achievable than previous mountaineers?

_____

_____

**Your prediction question:** _____

_____

**Your answer:** _____

_____

_____

How did you do?

# There is a Time

These wise words from the book of Ecclesiastes remind us that life is full of changes.

Read the incomplete sentences aloud and think about opposite responses to the words in bold. Use your prediction skills to fill in the gaps using words from the box below. Then answer the questions on page 29.

Use your knowledge about the world and the clues on the page to make your predictions.

There is a time for everything,

and a season for every activity under the heavens:

a time to be **born** and a time to **die**,

a time to **plant** and a time to **uproot**,

a time to **kill** and a time to _____,

a time to **tear down** and a time to _____,

a time to _____ and a time to **laugh**,

a time to **mourn** and a time to **dance**,

a time to **scatter stones** and a time to _____,

a time to **embrace** and a time to **refrain**,

a time to _____ and a time to **give up**,

a time to _____ and a time to **throw away**,

a time to _____ and a time to **mend**,

a time to **be silent** and a time to _____,

a time to _____ and a time to **hate**,

a time for _____ and a time for **peace**.

*Ecclesiastes 3, v 1–8*

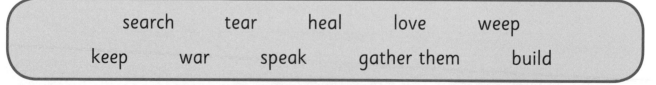

search     tear     heal     love     weep

keep     war     speak     gather them     build

1. What do you think the theme of this poem is? Tick the box next to your choice and then explain why you think that.

   ☐ endurance ☐ people ☐ life's journey ☐ wisdom

   _____

   _____

2. Why do you think there is 'a time to plant and a time to uproot'?

   _____

   _____

3. What do you predict happens to people who do not have time to laugh or dance? Why do you think that?

   _____

   _____

4. Why do you think 'a time to be silent' is important?

   _____

   _____

5. Complete the lines below using opposite words to the words in bold.

   a time to **be kind** and a time to be _____,

   a time to **serve** and a time to _____.

6. Explain when you think one of the actions you have suggested above might be appropriate.

   _____

   _____

How did you do?

# Book covers

Look at the book cover below. Circle clues in the title and design that suggest what the book might be about. Think about word and picture clues, characters, setting, style of font and what type of book it is.

Look for clues in the cover title and picture.

AFTER TOMORROW

'a fast-moving, incredibly exciting read' **Malorie Blackman**

SURVIVAL IS YOUR ONLY OPTION

GILLIAN CROSS

WINNER OF THE CARNEGIE MEDAL

Using the clues you have circled on the cover, answer these questions. Then ask and answer your own prediction question about the book.

**1.** What genre of book do you think this is? Why do you say that?

_____

_____

**2.** Identify four clues in the title and picture that you think suggest the time and setting of this story. Give your reasons for saying this.

    **a.** _____

    **b.** _____

    **c.** _____

    **d.** _____

**3.** From the information on the cover, what do you predict this story is about? Why do you say that?

_____

_____

**4.** What do you predict might happen next to the characters from the clues you have spotted? Give your reasons for saying that.

_____

_____

**Your prediction question:** _____

_____

**Your answer:** _____

_____

How did you do?

# The Disappearance of Tom Pile

Read this passage from *The Disappearance of Tom Pile* by Ian Beck. The text is about the early memories of Jack Carmody, an investigator of the supernatural.

Underline the clues that suggest what happened to Jack as a boy. How do these clues help you to predict what might have happened to him in his later life and why?

Link the clues and your knowledge about the world to predict what happened before and after.

It was one thing to see the patterns in things, to see through them. That was all connected to links and fast thinking. I suppose I was a bit like one of those adding machines most of the time. Seeing the lady in grey, though, that was different. Part of me sensed something about the hallway before I saw her. I knew there was something up: some part of my inner antennae told me. It was as if I had opened another undiscovered part of myself that afternoon. I realized, almost with a shock, that there were unexplained things, deep mysteries just at the edge of my understanding. I had somehow lifted a curtain on a new world.

Aunt Dolly drank her tea but I could tell she was troubled. What had just happened had scared her, and she wasn't someone who scared easily. It hadn't scared me, though – quite the opposite. I was excited by what else might be behind the curtain. Aunt Dolly never mentioned what I saw in that house in Hampstead. She didn't tell Lew the barber or anyone else – it worried her too much. I think she thought that I had somehow conjured up the lady in grey. As I got older I developed a keen sense in astronomy, and in the worlds beyond our own – which is how I came to be taken up by Captain Holloway.

When they discovered what I could do, I was soon whisked away from my local infant school. I was tutored at home instead, and that's when all the testing started. Aunt Dolly would regularly take me in to appointments in the West End. We went to impressive but fusty offices in places like Russell Square, where I was set difficult theorems and mathematical problems. We would visit various institutes where my intelligence was tested. It was all very friendly, but it involved us both getting dressed up and me having my hair strictly parted and smarmed down with horrible brilliantine, which Dolly bought at Lew's.

Use the clues you have underlined in the text and your prediction skills to help you answer the following questions.

**1.** What do you think Jack discovered when he was very young that might have shaped the rest of his life? Explain why you think that.

_____

_____

_____

_____

**2.** From the clues on the page do you predict that Jack saw a ghost in the house in Hampstead? Give your reasons for saying this.

_____

_____

_____

_____

**3.** Why do you think Aunt Dolly thought Jack had 'somehow conjured up the lady in grey'?

_____

_____

_____

_____

**4.** Why do you think Jack became a special investigator when he was older?

_____

_____

_____

**5.** Predict how Jack was later connected to Tom Pile, the boy in the picture. Why do you think this?

_____

_____

_____

Now ask and answer your own prediction question about Jack's story.

**Your prediction question:** _____

_____

**Your answer:** _____

_____

_____

_____

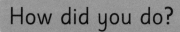 How did you do?

# What the Dickens

Read this passage about Charles Dickens, the famous Victorian writer. Highlight the 'who', 'what' and 'where' information in different coloured pens. What questions do you think PC Page might ask using this information?

PC Page is always looking out for literal clues. She notes down the **who**, **what** and **where** information that is right there on the page.

## What the Dickens?

(1812 – 1870 AD)

Charles John Huffam Dickens was born in Landport, Portsmouth, on 7th February 1812. He was the second of eight children born to John and Elizabeth Dickens, and described himself as a "very small and not-over-particularly-taken-care-of boy". Although not wealthy, the Dickens family was not poor. They moved to Chatham, Kent in 1817 and sent Charles to the fee paying William Giles' school in the area. Despite his youth, he was a frequent visitor to the theatre. He enjoyed Shakespeare, and claimed to have learned many things from watching plays.

By the time he was ten, the family had moved again; this time to London following the career of his father, John, who was a clerk in the Naval Pay Office. John had a poor head for money, but liked to impress people. As a result, he got into debt and was sent to Marshalsea Prison in 1824. His wife and most of the children joined him there (a common occurrence in those days before the Bankruptcy Act of 1869 abolished debtors' prisons). Charles, however, was put to work at Warren's Blacking Factory, where he labelled jars of boot polish.

Later in 1824, John's mother died and left enough money to her son to pay off his debts and get him released. John Dickens retired from the Navy Pay Office later that year and worked as a reporter for *The Mirror of Parliament*, where his brother-in-law was editor. He allowed Charles to leave Warren's Blacking

Factory, and go back to school. Charles's brief time at the factory continued to haunt him for the rest of his life. He later wrote:

"For many years, when I came near to Robert Warren's , in the Strand, I crossed over to the opposite side of the way, to avoid a certain smell of the cement they put upon the blacking corks, which reminded me of what I once was. My old way home by the borough made me cry, after my oldest child could speak."

Now circle the inference clues on the page that help you think more deeply about what is happening.

Use the information in the text on page 35 to help you answer the questions below. Tick the PC Page box next to the literal questions and tick the Text Detective box next to the inference questions.

Remember, **literal** answers are right there in the picture and text. **Inference** answers link to clues in the picture and text.

| Question | PC Page | Text Detective |
|---|---|---|
| **1.** Where was Charles Dickens born? <br> _____ | ☐ | ☐ |
| **2.** Did Charles think he was neglected by his parents sometimes? Explain how you know that. <br> _____ <br> _____ | ☐ | ☐ |
| **3.** Who was sent to prison because John Dickens had a poor head for money? <br> _____ | ☐ | ☐ |
| **4.** Why was Charles's education interrupted? <br> _____ | ☐ | ☐ |
| **5.** Did Charles enjoy his time in the factory? How do you know that? <br> _____ <br> _____ | ☐ | ☐ |
| **6.** What happened to Charles when his father retired from the Navy Pay Office? <br> _____ | ☐ | ☐ |

How did you do?

# Alienography or How To Spot an Alien Invasion

Think about how you know what is happening.

Read this extract from *Alienography* by Chris Riddell. Link the word clues with clues in the picture to explain what the character is wearing and why.

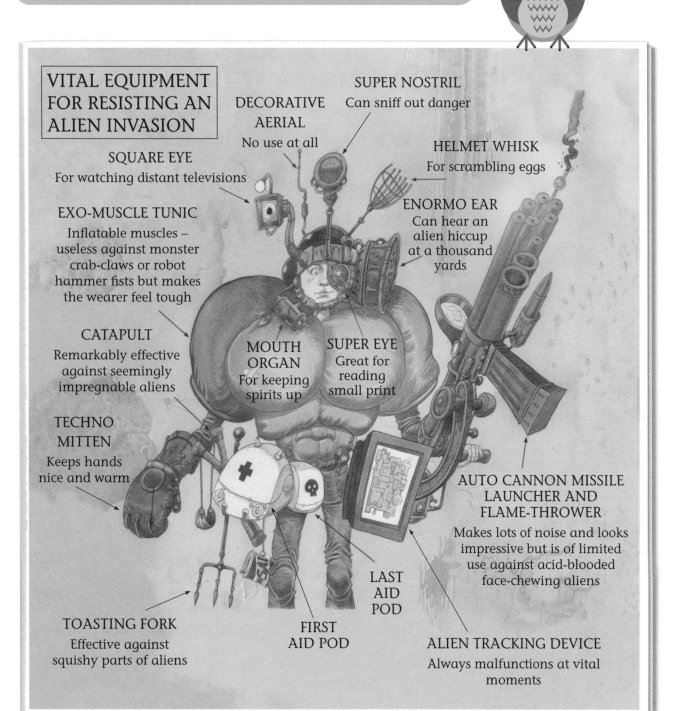

VITAL EQUIPMENT FOR RESISTING AN ALIEN INVASION

DECORATIVE AERIAL
No use at all

SUPER NOSTRIL
Can sniff out danger

HELMET WHISK
For scrambling eggs

SQUARE EYE
For watching distant televisions

ENORMO EAR
Can hear an alien hiccup at a thousand yards

EXO-MUSCLE TUNIC
Inflatable muscles – useless against monster crab-claws or robot hammer fists but makes the wearer feel tough

CATAPULT
Remarkably effective against seemingly impregnable aliens

MOUTH ORGAN
For keeping spirits up

SUPER EYE
Great for reading small print

TECHNO MITTEN
Keeps hands nice and warm

AUTO CANNON MISSILE LAUNCHER AND FLAME-THROWER
Makes lots of noise and looks impressive but is of limited use against acid-blooded face-chewing aliens

LAST AID POD

TOASTING FORK
Effective against squishy parts of aliens

FIRST AID POD

ALIEN TRACKING DEVICE
Always malfunctions at vital moments

Use the clues from the text on page 37 to help answer the questions below. Then ask and answer your own inference question about the text.

1.  Is the character dressed to defend himself against an attack from outer space? How do you know that?

    _____

    _____

2.  Explain how you know that some of the character's equipment is there mainly to boost his morale.

    _____

    _____

    _____

3.  Is some of the equipment the character is wearing rather unreliable and ineffective? How do you know that?

    _____

    _____

    _____

4.  Is the character carrying useful pieces of equipment to use against aliens? What evidence do you have for saying that?

    _____

    _____

    _____

**Your inference question:** _____

_____

**Your answer:** _____

_____

How did you do?

# Oliver Twist

Read this passage from the story *Oliver Twist* retold by Nicola Baxter. Circle clues that link together to explain what is happening and why.

**Workhouses** *were places where the poor did unpaid work in exchange for food and accommodation. There, conditions were harsh, and families were often split up.*

Oliver had to work as a (mourner.) His pale, (melancholy) face proved especially useful for children's funerals. Noah was a bully and said cruel things about Oliver's mother. A fight began, causing Mrs Sowerberry to lock Oliver in the coal cellar and send Noah for Mr Bumble. "It's not Madness, ma'am … it's Meat," claimed Mr Bumble, implying that Oliver was being treated too well.

Upset and angry, Oliver ran away. As he passed the workhouse, he met a dying child called Dick. "God bless you," said the poor boy – the first good wishes Oliver had ever received.

Arriving in London, exhausted and penniless, Oliver met another boy – the roistering, swaggering Artful Dodger, who took him to an old man called Fagin who seemed to have care of several boys. Warm, well fed and lulled by hot gin and water, Oliver slept deeply. He awoke to see Fagin gloating over a secret hoard of treasure. Noticing Oliver was awake, Fagin grabbed a knife as if to silence the boy for ever. Luckily, the old man calmed down. Later, Fagin taught his boys to pick pockets.

# Inference

Answer the questions below using 'because' to explain how you know the answer from the clues you have circled in the text. Then write your own inference question and answer.

Highlight the key words in the questions before you search for answers in the text and picture clues.

1. Was Oliver a convincing mourner at children's funerals? What evidence is there for saying that?

_____

_____

2. Was Noah largely to blame for getting Oliver into trouble with Mrs Sowerberry? How do you know?

_____

_____

3. Did Mr Bumble imply that Oliver was being spoilt by Mrs Sowerberry? Explain how you know.

_____

_____

4. Was Oliver feeling unhappy when he escaped his employers? How do you know that?

_____

_____

**Your inference question:** _____

_____

**Your answer:** _____

_____

How did you do?

# The River Singers

Read this extract from *The River Singers* by Tom Moorhouse. Circle the clues on the page that suggest **what** the characters are doing, **where** they are and **why**.

'Sylvan.'

Reluctantly he obeyed the warning tone in her voice and joined her, now with the others a little way up the bank. They were arranged in a circle around a towering patch of sweet-grass stems, squinting in the brightness, sniffing at the air.

'So, here you are. Welcome, my loves, to the Great River. But be careful out here. Every moment you spend in the open you need to be alert. If you hear anything odd – anything at all – freeze, be silent. If things go wrong, run, make it to the water or to the burrow and you'll be safe.'

She smiled. 'Well. Lecture over. Now that you are finally too big for milk, you will have to eat like the rest of us. I think it's about time you learned to feed yourselves. Like this.'

She grasped a thick sweet-grass stem and with a deft bite severed it from the base. Holding it upright, she ran it through her paws, expertly chopping it into lengths with her teeth, gnawing at the soft flesh and leaving aside the coarse outer parts. When she had finished there was a pile of discarded pieces at her feet.

'Go on,' she said. 'Try it.'

Sylvan grabbed for the largest stem he could find, making it shake far above him. Then he began chewing through the base. It was not easy. The outside was thick and dry, but the sweet juices from the middle flooded his mouth. He gnawed until his jaw ached, until only a few fibres held the giant plant upright, until… He realized his mistake only when the stem toppled sideways from his grasp and onto Fern's head.

'Ouch. Sylvan, will you please watch what you're doing?'

'Sorry.'

'You,' she said primly, 'are an idiot.' She turned back to her feeding. Sylvan wondered briefly about shoving her into the water. It probably wouldn't be a popular idea. Instead he abandoned his gigantic stem for a patch of smaller, new-grown woundworts. They tasted even better than the grass: less tough and a bit less bitter.

Write the **clues** in the box below. Two examples have been done for you.

Great River        learned to feed

Skim and scan the text on page 41 to find the words and phrases below. Answer the questions, using these clues and 'because' to explain how you know. Then ask and answer your own inference question.

Highlight the key words in the questions before you search for answers.

| | | |
|---|---|---|
| too big for milk | learned to feed yourselves | reluctantly |
| warning tone | soft flesh | coarse outer parts | expertly |
| leaving aside | outside was thick and dry | lecture |
| be careful out here | onto Fern's head | tasted even better |

1. Was Sylvan an independent little creature? How do you know that?

_____

_____

2. Had Sylvan and his siblings visited the Great River before? How do you know that?

_____

_____

3. Explain how you know that Sylvan and his brothers and sisters are no longer babies.

_____

_____

**Your inference question:** _____

_____

**Your answer:** _____

_____

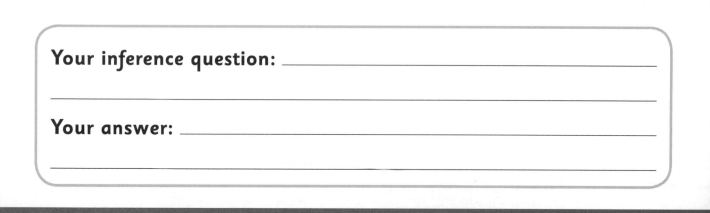

How did you do?

# Kite Flying

Think about the mood or message the poet wants to convey about kite flying.

Read this poem by Debjani Chatterjee. Underline the words that suggest the kite has human characteristics. Some examples have been done for you.

## Kite Flying

Soaring upwards to <u>play</u> among rain-clouds,
<u>Laughing with the elements</u>, <u>child of the wind</u>;
Clowning, uncaring, pioneering spirit,
Shaking your proud head, fluttering a shiny tail,
Fashioned of craft and simple cunning.
Riding the currents of airborne ecstasy,
You surf freedom's waves, sniff Monsoon magic.
Rebel, straining at the string of love and pain,
Do you acknowledge the fist that holds you tight,
The clutch of a child who is tied to the earth?
Do you feel the large bright eyes that follow you,
The heart uplifted with you, racing, daring,
Cart-wheeling and tumbling in the breeze;
Wild Pegasus, galloping, fun-frolicking,
Leaping and somersaulting among rain-clouds,
Laughing with the elements, child of the wind?

**Debjani Chatterjee**
India & UK

Circle unknown or difficult words and phrases in the poem. Use context clues to work out their meanings. Then answer the questions on page 44 and ask and answer your own clarification question about the poem.

Remember to underline the clues in the question before you search for the answers.

**1.** What does the term 'personification' mean?

_____

_____

**2.** Give an example of how the writer uses personification to good effect in this poem. Explain why you say that.

_____

_____

**3.** Choose a line from the poem that you like and explain why you like it.

_____

_____

_____

**4.** Explain what you think the poet means by 'Wild Pegasus, galloping, fun-frolicking'.

_____

_____

**5.** Why do you think the writer says the kite is a 'child of the wind'?

_____

_____

**Your clarification question:** _____

_____

**Your answer:** _____

_____

How did you do?

# Mysterious Traveller

Read the passage below from *Mysterious Traveller*. Identify the figurative language and underline the metaphors, similes and unusual phrases in the text. Some examples have been done for you.

Use your prediction skills and context clues to help clarify the meaning of the descriptive phrases in the text.

Issa, as usual, left his house before dawn and went to watch the <u>sun being born again</u>. At first it was a tiny red glimpse, as if someone had lit a fire among the distant hills. Slowly at first, then more quickly, <u>it grew and swelled</u> until it floated above the hills like a fat, shivery bubble. The colours of the desert came alive.

Issa's old eyes had watched thousands of dawns, but still it <u>seemed to him that each one was a miracle</u>. Each time, it lifted his heart. On this particular morning, however, the bottom edge of the sun was not as bright as usual. Blurry. Veiled. Issa squinted at it, then took a deep breath of the cold desert wind, testing its smell with his nose.

"Mmm," he murmured to himself. "Yes. Something has changed. There has been a storm in the hills, I think."

He turned to go back to his house. It was time for his prayers. Then he stopped.

Look for context clues in the questions on page 46 to help you clarify their meaning. Answer the questions and then ask and answer your own clarification question.

**Example:**

**Question:** Explain why it is an <u>effective use of metaphor</u> to compare <u>sunrise</u> to the '<u>sun being born again</u>'.

**Answer:** *It is an effective use of metaphor to compare sunrise to the 'sun being born again' because it suggests that each day is special and that with every sunrise there is a new beginning.*

1. Explain in your own words what figurative language is and why you think authors use this kind of language in their writing.

_____

_____

2. How does the author extend the idea of sunrise? Why is this effective?

_____

_____

_____

3. How do we know that dawn is a moving experience for Issa?

_____

4. Why did Issa think that the sunrise was different one morning? Explain in your own words.

_____

_____

5. Give another example of the author's use of figurative language in the passage and explain why you think it is effective.

_____

_____

_____

Your clarification question: _____

_____

Your answer: _____

_____

How did you do?

# Giant Winter

Read the poem below by John Foster. Identify examples of metaphors, similes and personification in the text. Underline the main clues in each line to help you clarify the overall meaning of each verse.

Use your prediction skills and context clues to help you clarify the meaning of the poetic language.

## Giant Winter

1
Giant Winter preys on the earth,
Gripping with talons of ice,
Squeezing, seeking a submission,
Tightening his grip like a vice.

2
Starved of sunlight, shivering trees
Are bent by his torturing breath.
The seeds burrow into the soil
Preparing to fight to the death.

3
Giant Winter sneers at their struggles,
Blows blizzards from his frozen jaws,
Ripples cold muscles of iron,
Clenches tighter his icicle claws.

4
Just as he seems to be winning,
Strength suddenly ebbs from his veins.
He releases his hold and collapses.
Giant spring gently takes up the reins.

5
Snarling, bitter with resentment,
Winter crawls to his polar den,
Where he watches and waits till it's time
To renew the battle again.

Using your knowledge of winter and the clues you have underlined in the poem, summarise the meaning of each verse in your own words.

| Verse | Summary |
|-------|---------|
| 1 | |
| 2 | |
| 3 | |
| 4 | |
| 5 | |

Answer these questions using the words you have underlined in the text and your summaries. The questions are continued on page 49.

1. What do you think the poet tells us about winter in this poem? Explain why you say that.

_____

_____

_____

_____

**2.** Explain why phrases like 'seeking a submission' and 'Tightening his grip like a vice' describe the power of winter so effectively.

_____

_____

_____

**3.** The poet gives winter almost human qualities. Give three examples.

**a.** _____

**b.** _____

**c.** _____

**4.** Do you think the poet suggests that seeds are like animals? Explain why you say this.

_____

_____

Now ask and answer your own clarification questions about the poem.

**Your clarification question:** _____

_____

**Your answer:** _____

_____

**Your clarification question:** _____

_____

**Your answer:** _____

_____

How did you do?

# From China to India

Read this extract from *The Great Explorers* by Stewart Ross and Stephen Biesty.

**Synonyms**: similar meaning
**Antonyms**: opposite meaning

Kublai Khan, the great emperor of China whom Marco Polo had admired so much, died in 1294. Seventy years later the Mongol dynasty he had founded collapsed. It was replaced by a native Chinese dynasty, the Ming (meaning "shining bright") dynasty.

The Great Khan had believed in sea power as a way to <u>defend</u> China, spread its power abroad and help foreign trade. His soldiers and merchants sailed the Indian Ocean (which they called the Western Sea) in gigantic ships known as junks. These vessels each had four masts and nine sails, and carried a crew of over 200 men.

In 1402, Zhu Di, the third Ming ruler, ascended the "dragon throne". Like Kublai Khan, he wanted his power and glory

to be recognised abroad. To achieve this, he determined to build a new and mighty "Treasure Fleet" of junks, and send it across the Western Sea to the great port of Calicut on India's west coast. On the way there, the fleet would stop to demand tax or "tribute" from the peoples and rulers it met, and to trade goods with them. The emperor also wanted his Treasure Fleet to tackle the dangerous pirates who lurked around the South China Sea.

Skim and scan the text to find words with **similar** meanings to the words in the box below (synonyms). Circle them as you find them and write them on the lines provided. One has been done for you.

**Synonyms**

**Example:** crumbled / collapsed

formidable/_____

heads of state/_____

buy and sell/_____

empire/_____

deal with/_____

skulked/_____

Now skim and scan the text to find words with **opposite** meanings to the words in the box below (antonyms). One has been done for you.

**Antonyms**

**Example:** attack / defend

disapproved of/_____

ignored/_____

home/_____

tame/_____

servant/_____

minute/_____

Underline the key words in the following questions that link to the **same**, **similar** or **opposite words** in the text. An example has been done for you. The questions are continued on page 52.

**Example:**

**Question:** Did the Great Khan's empire <u>crumble in his lifetime</u>? How do you know that?

**Answer:** No, the Great Khan's empire did not crumble in his lifetime because it <u>collapsed seventy years after his death</u>.

1.  Do you think Marco Polo disapproved of Kublai Khan? Why do you think that?

    _____

    _____

2.  Why do you think the junks that sailed the Indian Ocean in Kublai Khan's time carried soldiers and merchants?

    _____

    _____

3.  Which head of state was influenced by the success of a previous dynasty? How do you know that?

    _____

    _____

4.  Do you think the people who paid a 'tribute' were in awe of the formidable 'Treasure Fleet'? Why do you say that?

    _____

    _____

Now ask and answer your own clarification question about the text using a synonym or an antonym.

**Your clarification question:** _____

_____

**Your answer:** _____

_____

_____

How did you do?

# Way Home

Read this extract from *Way Home*, where a homeless boy and a cat are being pursued by a gang. Circle the clues in the picture and text that suggest what is happening and how the characters might be feeling. Then use these clues to answer the questions on page 54.

The boy leaps out into the road.
There's a blare of horns, a screaming of tongues and tyres.
But the cat with no name feels safe in the boy's jacket.
'Ahhhh,' the boy called Shane yells as he dives through.
They won't follow him here.

Remember, evaluation questions have no right or wrong answer, as long as you link your ideas to the information in the story.

1.  Explain what you think is happening and where the boy is.

    _____

    _____

2.  What does the picture tell you about how Shane is feeling? Why do you think he is feeling this way?

    _____

    _____

    _____

3.  Why do you think the cat feels safe in Shane's jacket?

    _____

4.  In the story, Shane is a homeless boy living on his own. How do you think it must feel to be living alone on the streets? Give your reasons.

    _____

    _____

    _____

Now ask and answer your own evaluation question about the text.

**Your evaluation question:** _____

_____

**Your answer:** _____

_____

How did you do?

# Great Expectations

Read this extract from a retelling of Charles Dickens's *Great Expectations*. Look for the 'who', 'what' and 'where' information. Then circle clues that explain what is happening and how the characters are feeling.

Remember to use your **literal** and **inference** skills, as well as personal experience, to think about the characters' feelings and actions in the story.

*Leg irons* were often used to restrain prisoners in Victorian times. Convicts were treated very harshly, and it was not uncommon for them to have their legs and arms shackled with rings of iron.

I ran without stopping to the forge where I lived with my sister and her husband, the blacksmith Joe Gargery. My sister was tall and bony and always wore a coarse apron. Joe was a sweet-tempered, foolish fellow. Wracked with fear, I could only pretend to eat my supper before going up to bed.

Early next morning, I crept downstairs and took from the pantry bread, cheese, mincemeat, brandy and a handsome pork pie. I stole a file from the forge and ran across the marshes towards the old Battery.

On my way, I observed a man dressed in grey, also with a leg iron, but he quickly vanished. After delivering my stolen goods, I returned home to find visitors arriving for Christmas lunch. There were Mr Hubble the wheelwright and his wife; Mr Wopsle the church clerk, and Joe's uncle, called Mr Pumblechook, a wealthy corn-chandler. I ate in terror of my thefts being noticed.

Then my sister went to get the pork pie.

Answer the questions below. Then ask and answer your own literal, inference and evaluation questions.

Think about the different question types.

**1.** What does Pip do in this part of the story following his encounter with a runaway convict on the marshes?

_____

**2.** Does Pip ensure everyone is still in bed before he delivers the stolen items? How do you know that?

_____

_____

**3.** Why do you think Pip 'could only pretend' to eat his supper?

_____

**Your literal question:** _____

**Your answer:** _____

**Your inference question:** _____

_____

**Your answer:** _____

_____

**Your evaluation question:** _____

_____

**Your answer:** _____

_____

How did you do?

# Christian Aid Week Appeal

What do you think the writer wants people to feel? Does the text influence your feelings? Why?

Look at the pictures and read the text below from the Christian Aid Week Appeal. The information asks the reader to support working mothers overseas. Circle the emotive language in the text and underline the facts.

CHRISTIAN AID WEEK APPEAL 2015

christian aid week

## Sometimes, even the strongest women need a little help...

Loko works 18 hours a day, but still struggles to feed her children. Will you help buy a cow for a hardworking mother?

At the end of a very exhausting day, Loko's shoulders ache and her feet are in agony. But what pains her most is hearing her children cry with hunger.

This Christian Aid Week, will you help buy a cow and give a hardworking mother like Loko a way to provide for her family?

Think of two different titles for this appeal. One should be factual and the other should be emotive.

Factual heading: _____

_____

Emotive heading: _____

_____

Remember to use personal experience, knowledge and evidence from the text.

Answer the questions below using clues from the appeal on page 57. Then ask and answer your own evaluation question.

1. What do you think the message is behind this appeal? Why do you think that?

_____

_____

_____

2. How does the slogan at the top of the appeal text make you feel? Explain why it has this effect on you.

_____

_____

_____

_____

3. Who do you think this appeal is aimed at? Explain why you think that.

_____

_____

_____

Your evaluation question: _____

_____

Your answer: _____

_____

_____

How did you do?

# Dead Man's Cove

Read this extract from *Dead Man's Cove* by Lauren St John. Circle the clues in the text that might explain how the character is feeling and why. Use these clues to help you answer the questions on page 60. Then ask and answer your own evaluation question.

They came for her at 6.47am. Laura made a note of the time because she'd been waiting for this moment for eleven years, one month and five days and she wanted always to remember it – the hour her life began.

It was still dark but she was already awake. Already packed. The sum total of her possessions had been laid out in her suitcase with a military neatness – two of everything except underwear and books, of which there were seven apiece. One pair of knickers for each day of the week, as ordered by matron, but not enough novels by half. Then again, Laura wasn't sure how many would be enough. When you spent your whole life waiting, books became like windows. Windows on the world; on the curious workings of the human mind; on shipwrecks, audacious jewel thieves and lights that signalled in the night. On giant hounds that roamed fog-wreathed moors, on magical tigers and savage bears, on incredible feats of survival and courage.

Laura sighed and pulled back the curtain beside her bed. Her real window didn't open onto any of those things. Once it had faced the rolling, flower-filled landscape that had given the Sylvan Meadows Children's Home its name, but that was before a Health and Safety official decided that nature presented a danger. As a result, Laura looked out onto a car park and a tarmac playground with a couple of swings.

Before the hedge was a suburb of identical brown brick houses, now covered in snow. It was a vista of unrelenting dullness.

Remember to underline the key words in the questions.

**1.** Do you think this story might be about adventure and new horizons? Explain why you say that.

_____

_____

**2.** Do you think Laura was feeling excited when they came for her at 6.47am? Why do you think that?

_____

_____

**3.** Why do you think Laura had only a few possessions?

_____

_____

**4.** How do you think Laura felt about the view from her window at the children's home? Explain why you say that.

_____

_____

**5.** Do you think Laura was passionate about books? Why do you say that?

_____

_____

**Your evaluation question:** _____

_____

**Your answer:** _____

_____

How did you do?

# The Steadfast Tin Soldier

Look at the picture and read this extract from *The Steadfast Tin Soldier* by Hans Christian Andersen. Then answer the questions on page 62.

WHEN morning came and the children were up again, the tin soldier was placed on the window ledge. The goblin may have been responsible, or perhaps a draught blowing through – anyhow, the window suddenly swung open, and out fell the tin soldier, all the three storeys to the ground. It was a frightful fall! His leg pointed upwards, his head was down, and he came to a halt with his bayonet stuck between the paving stones.

**1.** What is the problem for the tin soldier at the beginning of the story?

_____

**2.** Who placed the tin soldier on the window ledge?

_____

**3.** Was the window ledge a safe place to leave the tin soldier? How do you know that?

_____

_____

**4.** 'The goblin may have been <u>responsible</u>' for the tin soldier's fall. Tick the box that has a similar meaning to the word 'responsible' here.

**synonym (similar):** ☐ faultless    ☐ answerable    ☐ sensible

**5.** How do you think the tin soldier felt when he landed upside down? Give your reasons for saying that.

_____

_____

Now write your own question and answer. Tick the box to show which type of question it is.

☐ literal question    ☐ inference question    ☐ evaluation question

**Your question:** _____

_____

**Your answer:** _____

_____

How did you do?

# Discover animal tracks and signs

Look at the pictures and read the following information about animal tracks and signs. Then answer the questions on page 64.

## Discover animal tracks and signs

Look for animal footprints in mud, sand or snow.

Owls spit out bits (pellets) of their prey they can't digest.

Look for pine cones that have been stripped by hungry squirrels.

Molehills are signs that moles are nearby.

Look under hedges and in banks for rabbit holes.

Birds shed their feathers when they are damaged.

If the trail is continuous, it's a slug. If broken, it's a snail.

Mammals can leave flattened grass in their tracks.

Animal fur can get caught on barbed wire and fences.

Look for hedgehog poo with bits of beetles in it.

Nests are a surefire sign that birds are breeding. Hooray!

Song thrushes leave behind broken snail shells after meals.

www.wildlifewatch.org.uk

wildlife watch

THE wildlife TRUSTS

Illustrations. Corinne Welch © Copyright Royal Society of Wildlife Trusts 2015

1. List three tracks or signs that indicate animals are nearby.

   a. _____  b. _____  c. _____

2. What leaves a continuous slimy trail wherever it goes?

   _____

3. Name a part of the hedgehog's diet. Explain how you know this.

   _____

   _____

4. Do birds sometimes leave evidence behind them when they are injured? How do you know?

   _____

5. Explain what 'pellets' are.

   _____

6. Describe the animal tracks and signs that you would most like to find. Explain why.

   _____

   _____

Now write your own question and answer. Tick the box to show which type of question it is.

☐ literal question   ☐ inference question   ☐ evaluation question

**Your question:** _____

**Your answer:** _____

_____

How did you do?

# A Christmas Carol

Read this extract from the graphic book version of *A Christmas Carol* by Charles Dickens. Then answer the questions on page 66. Think about the different question types as you work through them.

© Classical Comics

1. Who is this passage about, what are they doing and where are they?

_____

2. What is Scrooge doing?

_____

3. Why is the clerk using the flame of a candle to try to warm himself?

_____

4. Why do you think the clerk does not ask his employer for more coal to put on his fire?

_____

_____

5. 'In which effort, not being a man of strong imagination, he failed.' What do you think the author means by this?

_____

_____

Now write your own question and answer. Tick the box to show which type of question it is.

☐ literal question   ☐ inference question   ☐ evaluation question

**Your question:** _____

_____

**Your answer:** _____

_____

How did you do?

# Weather

Read this information about weather. Then answer the questions on page 68. Think about the different question types as you read.

## Weather

There are lots of different kinds of weather. It can be rainy, snowy, sunny or windy. The three main things that make the weather happen are the Sun, the air and water.

The Sun gives out heat.

The air moves to make wind.

Water makes rain and snow.

**4.** The water droplets bump into other droplets and join together to make clouds.

### Rainy days

The amount of water in the world is always the same. Rain isn't new water. Follow the numbers to find out where rain comes from.

**3.** Up in the sky, it's cooler and the gas turns back into tiny water droplets.

**5.** As more water is added, the droplets get bigger and heavier and fall as rain.

**2.** The water turns into water vapor, a gas which we can't see, and rises up into the sky.

**6.** The rain falls down to the ground where it flows back into seas, lakes and rivers.

**1.** The Sun heats up the water in seas, lakes, rivers, and snow on mountain tops.

1. What is this text about? Retell the main points in your own words.

   _____

   _____

2. What are the three main things that make weather happen?

   _____

3. Is rain recycled water? How do you know that?

   _____

4. 'The water turns into water vapour' and becomes invisible when it heats up. Which of these words do you think describes this process?

   ☐ evaporation          ☐ condensation          ☐ distillation

5. Do you think weather plays an important part in our daily lives? Explain why you say that.

   _____

   _____

Now write your own question and answer. Tick the box to show which type of question it is.

☐ literal question      ☐ inference question      ☐ evaluation question

Your question: _____

_____

Your answer: _____

_____

How did you do?

# Tinder

Read this passage from *Tinder* by Sally Gardner. Then answer the questions on pages 70 and 71.

I tried to crawl away, sure that I was intended for the great pot that hung over the fire. He looked at me. Only then could I make out the fellow. His animal face was no more than a headpiece that fell, skin and fur, over his ears. Underneath, his face was white as ice, his eyes as red as flames. He had no beard upon his chin.

'Who are you?' I asked.

He took a cup of liquid from the pot and told me to drink.

'What is it?'

'I can do this with you awake or with you asleep,' said the half-beast half-man.

'Do what? Kill me?'

That made him laugh.

'Kill you?' he said. 'The bullet in your side has a mind to do that for you without my help. It needs to come out if it's not to poison you completely. As for the wound in your shoulder – too much blood has been lost. Drink.'

'Why would you want to help me?'

'Drink, Otto Hundebiss, drink.'

I did and my eyes became heavy. Before I thought to ask him how he knew my name I was engulfed in pain so overwhelming that it chased me from my body. I was aware of floating out of myself. Below me lay a young man, broken on the carpet of leaves. I could clearly see the half-beast half-man put his hand into the very flesh of him. Yet, surprising as it seemed, I felt nothing, detached as I was and at peace, unlike any peace I had ever known.

Think about the different question types. Underline the clues in the questions to help you answer them.

1. Who is this story about, what are they doing and where are they?

_____

_____

2. Where are Otto's wounds?

_____

3. Does Otto decide that the creature is part-animal when he looks more closely at him? Explain how you know that.

_____

_____

4. Does Otto think he is in danger? How do you know?

_____

_____

5. Why do you think the creature gives Otto the cup of liquid to drink?

_____

_____

6. What do you think Otto means when he says 'I was engulfed in pain so overwhelming that it chased me from my body'.

_____

_____

**7.** Do you think Otto is frightened after the drink takes effect? Why do you say that?

_____

_____

**8.** What do you think Otto means when he says 'detached as I was'?

_____

_____

**9.** What do you think becomes of Otto in the end? Why do you say that?

_____

_____

**10.** Do you think Otto's character might have been in search of peace throughout this story? Explain why you think that.

_____

_____

Now write your own question and answer. Tick the box to show which type of question it is.

☐ literal question    ☐ inference question    ☐ evaluation question

**Your question:** _____

_____

**Your answer:** _____

_____

How did you do?

# Deadly Deserts

Read this information about living in the desert. Then answer the questions on page 73.

Deserts are such desperate places, it's a wonder anyone lives there at all. But despite the dreadful heat and drought, about 650 million people call deserts home. Hardy, or what? So how on earth do these desert dwellers handle the harsh conditions? A few years ago, Wanda spent some time with the Bedouin people of the Arabian Desert and found out just how they keep their cool.

### HORRIBLE HEALTH WARNING

Surviving in the desert is no picnic. Forget tucking into your sand-wiches. In the desert, food takes second place. You can go for weeks without eating but without water, you'd be dead in two days. To stay alive, you need to drink at least a bucket of water a day.

## NOTES FROM MY TRAVELS
### by Wanda

#### THE BEDOUIN

The Bedouin people mainly live in Arabia and North Africa. Their Arabic name is Bedu, which means 'people of the desert'.

The Bedouin are nomads, which means they're constantly on the move. They shift from place to place in search of food and water for themselves and their animals.

With all that moving, they need a home that's easy to put up and take down and that fits neatly on the back of a camel. And what could be better than a nice, snug tent made from camel's hair or sheep's wool?

When it comes to desert dress, the Bedouin know what to wear. And keeping cool's what counts. Their loose, flowing robes are ideal for letting air circulate and their long headdresses keep the sand and sun out.

The Bedouin are famous for their hospitality. They'll always give guests a meal and a place to stay. But watch your manners. Turn down a cup of coffee and you'll offend the whole family.

**1.** What is the main problem with living in the desert?

_____

**2.** Who lives a nomadic life in the harsh conditions of the Arabian Desert?

_____

**3.** Is food the main priority in the desert? Explain how you know.

_____

_____

**4.** What do you think the main occupation of the Bedouin people is? Explain why you say that.

_____

_____

**5.** 'The Bedouin are famous for their <u>hospitality</u>.' Tick the box that you think best describes the meaning of the word 'hospitality'.

☐ rudeness ☐ friendliness ☐ shyness

Now write your own question and answer. Tick the box to show which type of question it is.

☐ literal question ☐ inference question ☐ evaluation question

**Your question:** _____

_____

**Your answer:** _____

_____

How did you do?

# Roof Toppers

Read this passage from the beginning of *Roof Toppers* by Katherine Rundell. Then answer the questions on pages 75 and 76.

On the morning of its first birthday, a baby was found floating in a cello case in the middle of the English Channel.

It was the only living thing for miles. Just the baby, and some dining-room chairs, and the tip of a ship disappearing into the ocean. There had been music in the dining hall, and it was music so loud and so good that nobody had noticed the water flooding in over the carpet. The violins went on sawing for some time after the screaming had begun. Sometimes the shriek of a passenger would duet with a high C.

The baby was found wrapped for warmth in the musical score of a Beethoven symphony. It had drifted almost a mile from the ship, and was the last to be rescued. The man who lifted it into the rescue boat was a fellow passenger, and a scholar. It is a scholar's job to notice things. He noticed that it was a girl, with hair the colour of lightening, and the smile of a shy person.

Think of night-time with a speaking voice. Or think how moonlight might talk, or think of ink, if ink had vocal chords. Give those things a narrow aristocratic face with hooked eyebrows, and long arms and legs, and that is what the baby saw as she was lifted out of her cello case and up into safety. His name was Charles Maxim, and he determined, as he held her in his large hands – at arm's length, as he would a leaky flowerpot – that he would keep her.

Think about the different question types. Underline the clues in the questions to help you answer them.

1. What is this passage about? Retell the main points in your own words.

_____

_____

_____

2. What was the baby girl wrapped up in to keep her warm?

_____

3. Do you predict that there may have been some loss of life when the ship sank? Why do you think that?

_____

_____

4. Why do you think the baby was the last to be rescued?

_____

_____

5. Do you think the musicians kept on playing as the ship sank? How do you know that?

_____

_____

6. Why do you think the baby might have been put in a cello case?

_____

_____

**7.** Why do you think the author compares the baby girl's hair with 'the colour of lightning' and her smile to that of a shy person?

_____

_____

**8.** 'Think of night-time with a speaking voice.' Explain what you think the author means by this when she talks about what the baby saw.

_____

_____

**9.** Why do you think Charles held the baby at arm's length like 'a leaky flowerpot'?

_____

_____

**10.** 'Sometimes the shriek of a passenger would duet with a high C.' Why has the author chosen these words? How do they make you feel?

_____

_____

_____

Now write your own question and answer. Tick the box to show which type of question it is.

☐ literal question    ☐ inference question    ☐ evaluation question

**Your question:** _____

**Your answer:** _____

_____

How did you do?

# Jurassic Park: All in the genes

Read this information about recreating extinct animals. Then answer the questions on pages 78 and 79.

All in the genes

# Jurassic Park

Could we bring back the dinosaurs? They did it in the movies, but is it technically possible? And do we *really* want to?

## Back to the bird

**Re-creating an extinct animal** is much harder in real life than it is in the movies. Scientists face a number of *problems*, the main one being that DNA, an animal's genetic code, does not survive for long once the animal is dead. **Most fossils**, including those of the dinosaurs, *are too old to recover any DNA.* One way around the problem would be to start with an existing animal and work backwards. We know that birds are descended from the dinosaurs, so it may be possible to RE-CREATE A DINO by switching genes on or off in birds. Scientists have already managed to make bird embryos grow longer tails and feathers on their scaly legs.

*But what would we do with a DINOSAUR even if we did manage to grow a new one?*

GRRR!!

THE BIGGEST BIRD EGG YOU COULD USE TO MAKE A DINOSAUR IS THAT OF AN OSTRICH. THIS COULD GROW A DINO THE SIZE OF VELOCIRAPTOR.

*Tyrannosaurus rex* was one of the most fearsome predators that ever lived.

Teeth forming in the beak of a chicken.

## Rare as hen's teeth

Birds have not had teeth for 70 million years, but researchers have found them in the embryos of mutant chickens. It is thought birds lost their teeth to grow beaks instead, but still have the potential to make them. The teeth were just like those of a crocodile – another relative of the dinosaur.

Think about the different question types. Underline the clues in the questions to help you answer them.

1. How do scientists think we could solve the problem of recreating extinct animals?

_____

_____

_____

2. Name a living relative of the dinosaur that has similar teeth to those of the earliest birds' teeth?

_____

3. Is DNA easy to recover from most fossils, including those of dinosaurs? How do you know?

_____

_____

4. Do you predict that scientists will find a way soon to recreate an extinct animal? What evidence is there for saying that?

_____

_____

_____

5. Do you think it is morally right or safe to try to recreate a dinosaur? Why do you say that?

_____

_____

_____

**6.** Tick the box that you think best describes what an embryo is.

☐ growth          ☐ cells          ☐ foetus

**7.** Do chickens still have the potential to grow teeth? How do you know?

_____

_____

**8.** Predict why you think birds lost their teeth to grow beaks instead.

_____

_____

_____

_____

**9.** 'Researchers have found them in the embryos of <u>mutant</u> chickens.'
What does 'mutant' mean? Tick the box that you think best describes
the meaning of the word.

☐ rebellious          ☐ malformed          ☐ unchanged

Now write your own question and answer. Tick the box to show which
type of question it is.

☐ literal question    ☐ inference question    ☐ evaluation question

**Your question:** _____

_____

**Your answer:** _____

_____

_____

How did you do?

# Progress chart

Tick (✔) Ollie when you have completed the chapter.

1 Retelling

2 Literal questioning

3 Prediction

4 Inference

5 Clarification

6 Evaluation

7 Review

Well done! You have now completed the Comprehension workbook for ages 10–11.